HONEY

A Gift from Nature

Kane/Miller
BOOK PUBLISHERS

My father is a beekeeper.

When spring arrives in the mountains, the animals awaken, and my father's bees are busy.

At our house, there is bread and honey for breakfast, and I wonder about the honey, and the bees, and the mountains. "Dad," I ask, "May I come with you to see the bees?"

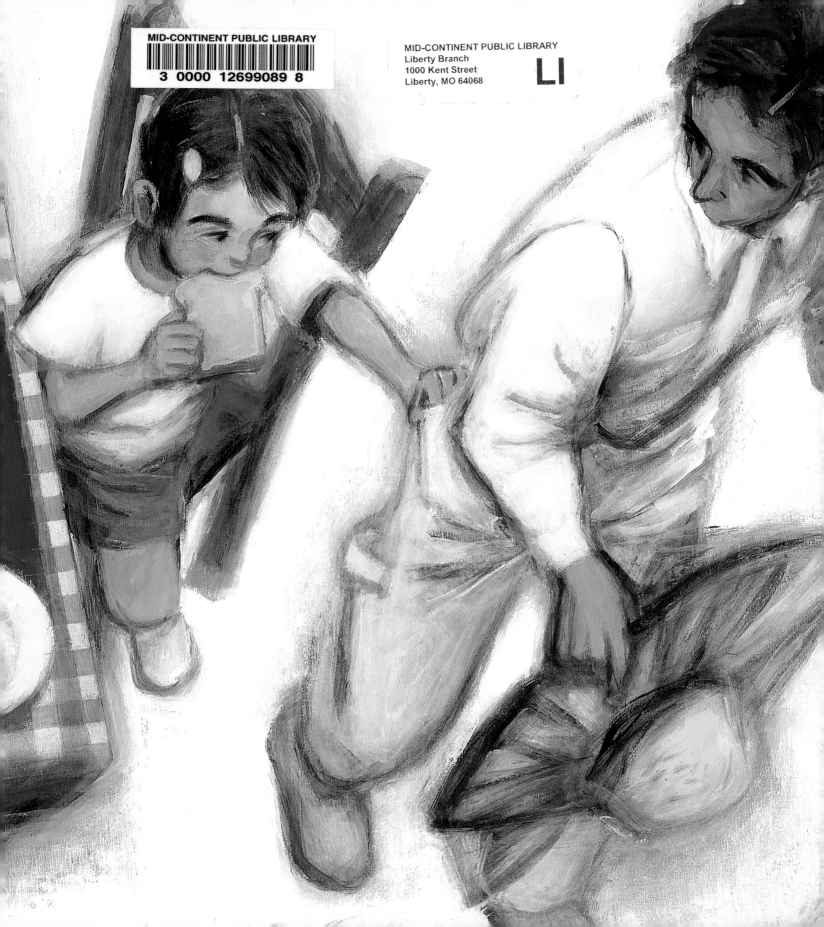

We drive into the mountains where my father keeps the hives. The chestnut trees are in full bloom, and they seem to bow and dance in the breeze. The bees fly in and out of the hives, and their buzzing makes it feel almost like the air around us is moving too.

The bees return to the hives looking fat and heavy with nectar. There are so many chestnut trees and so many flowers that their legs are covered with pollen and their stomachs are very, very full. Their bodies are tiny, but strong.

I watch from a distance until my father opens the lids of the hives and fills them with smoke.

The smoke will calm and confuse the bees, making it safe to come closer.

I put on my hat and veil (just in case), and join my father.

He slowly lifts one of the frames from the inside of the hive. The bees are swarming, crawling over both sides. "Put your hand near them," he tells me. Slowly, I gather my courage and hold out my palm. I can feel the heat.

My father shakes the frame, and the bees fall off, back into the hive. The hexagon-shaped honeycomb fills the frame, with small plugs of beeswax holding in the honey.

How does the nectar turn into honey?

After the bees return, they transfer the nectar they have collected to the mouths of the bees that remain in the hive.

These bees add enzymes from their bodies to the nectar. (An enzyme is a protein produced by a living thing that causes a chemical reaction.) The enzymes cause the water in the nectar to evaporate as it passes through the bees' bodies. Then the nectar is stored in a cell of the honeycomb.

Flap

Flap

The enzymes continue to react, and the bees use their wings to fan the comb and remove even more water from the processed nectar. Over time, it becomes honey.

A bee can make about half a teaspoon of honey in its lifetime.

Now the work to remove the honey from the frames can begin.
"Honey is the most precious thing to bees," my father says,
"so we take just a little in exchange for taking care of them."

He gently knocks off the few bees left on the frame, then carefully
slices down the side, cutting off the plugs of wax. Then I take the
frames and place them, one after the other, in the centrifuge.

They're heavy with honey.
We're going to collect a lot.

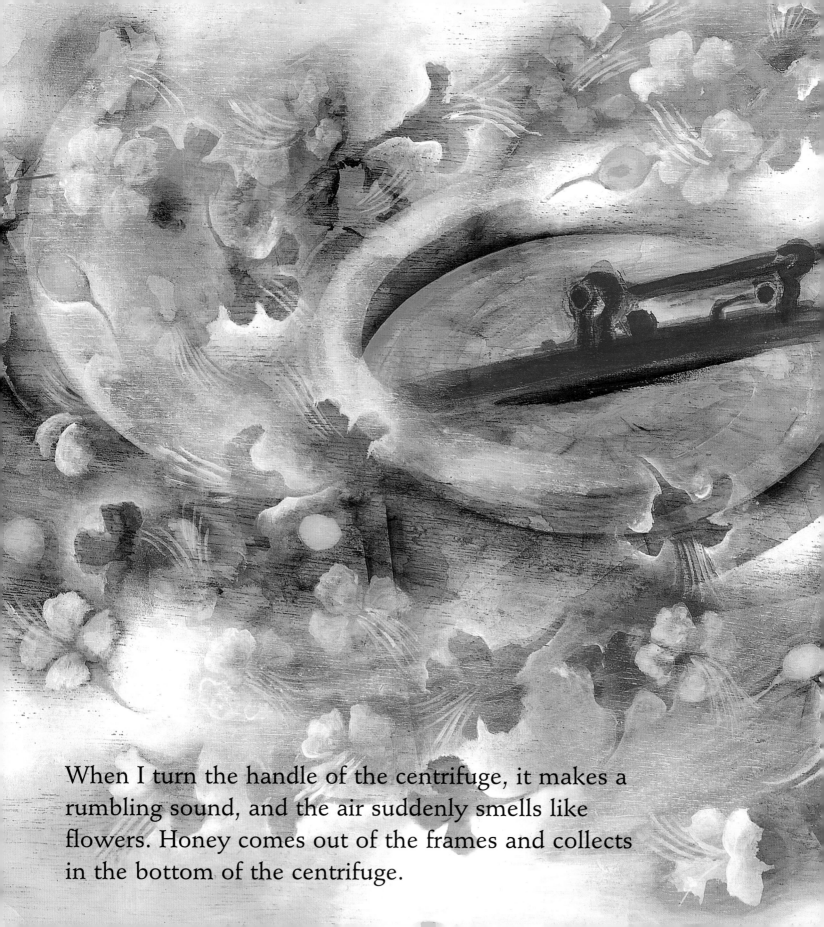

When I turn the handle of the centrifuge, it makes a rumbling sound, and the air suddenly smells like flowers. Honey comes out of the frames and collects in the bottom of the centrifuge.

It smells good!
I'll get some bread.

Turn the tap, and...
It looks delicious.

Later, we'll have raspberry and black locust, as the trees bloom in turn, and the bees gather the nectar.

At the end of summer, during the rains, wasps attack one of my father's beehives.

Wasps are one of the most feared enemies of bees.

Autumn is another.
And then there are the bears.

My father told me bears will completely destroy beekeepers'
hives if they are left unprotected.
Bears love honey.

In the winter, my father goes to the mountains to cover the hives with straw. The bees will stay in the center of the hives and wait out the cold winter until spring arrives once more.

I like that the honey tastes different, depending on which flowers
the bees used.

Chestnut

Apple

And I like that I know how honey is made.
I don't have to wonder – I've seen it!

Thistle

Buckwheat

Honey is a wonderful gift from nature.